PERAMBU

Jan and Geoff Swift

SHIRE PUBLICATIONS

Published in Great Britain in 2010 by Shire Publications
Ltd, Midland House, West Way, Botley, Oxford OX2 0PH,
United Kingdom.
44-02 23rd St, Suite 219, Long Island City, NY 11101,
USA.

E-mail: shire@shirebooks.co.uk   ww.shirebooks.co.uk

© 2008 Jan and Geoff Swift; reprinted 2010.

A CIP catalog record for this book is available from the
British Library.

Shire Library no. 472   •   ISBN-13: 978 0 74780 684 4

Jan and Geoff Swift have asserted their right under the
Copyright, Designs and Patents Act, 1988,
to be identified as the authors of this book.

Designed by Ken Vail Graphic Design, Cambridge, UK and
typeset in Perpetua and Gill Sans.
Printed in China through Worldprint.

10 11 12 13 14   11 10 9 8 7 6 5 4 3 2

ACKNOWLEDGEMENTS

We are grateful to Jonathan Coate, at the Willows &
Wetlands Visitors Centre, Somerset, for allowing us to
photograph the carriage on page 9, and to Silver Cross for
the pictures on page 63.

All other perambulators in the book belong to the authors'
collection.

COVER IMAGE
An Edwardian carriage perambulator.

TITLE PAGE IMAGE
An Edwardian period photograph.

CONTENTS PAGE IMAGE
A Victorian doll's mailcart with an Armand Marseille 390
doll.

Shire Publications is supporting the Woodland Trust, the UK's leading woodland conservation charity, by funding the dedication of trees.

CONTENTS

PREFACE   4

INTRODUCTION   5

EARLY CARTS AND CARRIAGES   6

VICTORIAN INDUSTRY   9

EDWARDIAN STYLE   25

BETWEEN THE WARS   37

A POST-WAR REVIVAL   51

THE WAY FORWARD   63

INDEX   64

PREFACE

W E hope that this book will give an enjoyable insight into the variety of baby carriages that have been used in times past. Surprisingly, for such an important part of our heritage, there are very few books on the subject.

Prams, Mailcarts and Bassinets, written by the late Jack Hampshire, though no longer in print, is the major work and gives the definitive history of baby carriages. The core of his once very large collection of prams is now held by the Jack Hampshire Trust and is on public view. There is no dedicated website but information can be found at www.babyequipmentcomplete.co.uk/museum which provides pictures of prams at the museum.

Left:
A mid-Victorian bassinet made for Harrods.

Right:
An Edwardian carriage pram.

Left:
A deep-bodied pram, c.1930.

Right:
A 1950s Marmet coach-built pram.

INTRODUCTION

THE British perambulator is the sole focus of this book, which charts its development from 1840 to the present day. The long-held reputation of British prams for design and craftsmanship is widely recognised and they have been exported throughout the world since Victorian times. The emergence and popularity of dolls' prams, often made by the same manufacturers as their full-size counterparts, will be considered in parallel. The terms *full* and *doll's* will generally be used to distinguish between the two sizes.

The book is divided into five main chapters, which deal with the significant periods in the development of the perambulator industry.

Prams have been part of our social fabric for more than 150 years. They reflect and have influenced the times in which they were made, being both a fashion statement and the means by which the future generation could be protected and transported. Medical opinion, in particular, has exerted a strong influence on their design. The changes in shape, style, methods of manufacture and materials used in construction, as will be seen, are all indicators in deciding when a pram was made.

A nostalgic Victorian postcard showing a girl with her toy mailcart.

Perambulators represent an experience we all share both as babies, for those who can remember, and later as parents and grandparents. Most people have affectionate memories of these encounters, and prams seem to carry with them their own tantalising secrets of past occupants and times.

EARLY CARTS AND CARRIAGES

THE notion of a carriage designed to carry an infant must always have seemed attractive but perambulators, as we know them, did not appear until the first years of Queen Victoria's reign, around 1840. Much earlier examples are recorded both in paintings and in museum exhibits but all were carriages individually commissioned and made by craftsmen or coachbuilders. Such carriages were the prerogative of the wealthy and for most other people the infant was either carried or, for ease, strapped to the mother. The majority of people travelled very little in the eighteenth century, life revolving around local work and the home. Families were large, so there was usually an older sibling to share the burden of the baby. In view of the cramped living conditions of the majority, let alone the state of the highways, a child's wheeled carriage would not have seemed a very practical proposition, however desirable.

The wealthy, however, living in large houses with extensive grounds, having long drives and pathways, could indulge in a small carriage especially made by the estate carpenter for the children. These park carriages were based on, and closely resembled, the horse-drawn carriages of the day and were pulled around the grounds by the nanny or the servants. These carriages were prohibited by law from being used on the public highway and were created purely for the pleasure of enjoying the estate.

Left:
A fine example of a hand-pulled carriage. The 3 feet long seating compartment is arranged to carry two small children.

Right:
A Victorian photograph of a young child in the same carriage.

The noblest families could also aspire to a fine and ornate, almost ceremonial carriage in which their cherished children could be paraded. Such carriages often took the form of a scallop shell and were embellished with the family emblems. The elaborate carving was gilded and plush velvet was used for the upholstered single seat. Unlike the park carriages, they were pushed from behind.

The majority of the population had to be content with any form of transport that could be utilised to carry children. Growing babies can be heavy to carry and toddlers get tired, so practical solutions were no doubt found. Small four-wheeled general purpose carts, like the one from the Somerset Levels illustrated, were often used – indeed, there are stories, from the elderly original owner of the cart, of it still being used for this purpose well into the Victorian era.

Interestingly, hand-pushed three-wheeled carriages were already being used to carry elderly or infirm adult passengers. Bath chairs, as they were called, were first seen in 1750 and had become popular by the end of the eighteenth century. They must have attracted the attention of many a child, who was possibly allowed to share the seat with an elderly grandparent. The potential of a child's size version of this three-wheeled chair must surely have been visualised.

It would, however, be left to Victorian enterprise and industry to find the solution to the obvious need for a generally available child's carriage.

A small general-purpose cart with a body length of 30 inches. The construction and craftsmanship are equal in quality to what was seen in full-size wagons.

VICTORIAN INDUSTRY

THE early years of Queen Victoria's reign mark the starting point in considering a history of British perambulators. During the 1840s a few manufacturers independently began, on a small scale, the production of carriages for children. Some of these manufacturers were already involved with the making of Bath chairs and this must have influenced their ideas.

The first small carriages consisted of a 'chair' on a simple chassis, supported by three wheels, which was pushed from behind. The invention offered a practical solution to the problem of transporting children and in 1846 attracted the attention of the young Queen Victoria, who purchased three such carriages for her growing family. Her interest and patronage helped to increase their popularity and made them fashionable in the privileged wealthy society of the day.

Significantly, these small carriages offered parents, for the first time, a purpose-built product that they could choose and purchase from a selection available in shops.

The first three-wheeled carriages were, however, just a small beginning to a period that produced many more innovations, including, in due course, a flat-bed pram for babies. Such was the progress made that the perambulator available at the end of the nineteenth century was, in concept, so advanced that it would be influencing pram design for many decades to come.

The pram had, in the same sixty-year period, moved from a position of a fashionable status symbol for the privileged few to being affordable for the growing number of wealthy people in late Victorian society.

Opposite:
A fine late Victorian mailcart. A contemporary advertisement described a similar model as most suitable for a christening present.

Below:
A very early child's carriage with wooden wheels, c.1850 (seat restored).

A young child in an early example of a three-wheeled carriage. The picture is a little indistinct as it comes from an ambrotype image on glass.

The early manufacturers all produced carriages of similar pattern with three wooden wheels. The seats were upholstered in buttoned leather cloth and safety straps were fitted to prevent the child falling out. Storm aprons could be fitted and a folding fringed sun canopy offered an added refinement. The carriages were intended to carry a child only in a sitting position. Exposure to fresh air was not considered advisable for babies at this time, so the limitations in use of these carriages would not have been seen as important.

Centre left and left:
A child's folding carriage from the 1850s, labelled 'T. Trotmans, Makers by Royal Patent', a company which was to become one of the leading pram makers. The canopy is stamped 'PRIZE MEDAL, Scowens patent, 1858, Makers to Her Majesty the Queen, Stoke Newington.'

The three-wheeled perambulator for a child generally remained the only kind available for more than thirty years. The name 'perambulator' was by now already being used to describe a child's carriage. The only major refinement in this period was the patenting and production by a Mr Frampton, one of the early pioneers in perambulator manufacture, of more easily produced and durable metal wheels with solid rubber tyres. The move away from craftsman-made wooden wheels offered the possibility of a less expensive production process. The wheels also gave the added benefit of a smoother ride.

There were some changes in appearance, but the basic concept otherwise changed very little in this time. Improvement in production methods, however, resulted in a reduction in price, further increasing the customer base.

These popular carriages would, by the end of the era, have four wheels and be called *victorias* – a reference to the horse-drawn carriages in which adults rode to the park.

Above: A doll's model that is a particularly detailed copy of the full-size version. It gives a good illustration of the kind of carriages available in the mid-Victorian period.

Below: The early doll's model has bold coach lines in red and yellow on the wheels and body. The wheels have wooden hubs and spokes and the rims are bent metal. The hood has an unusual striped silk lining which appears to be original.

An early 'basket on wheels' bassinet.

The dominance of the three-wheeled carriage was broken in the early 1880s when the demand for a flat-bed pram to carry babies was satisfied. The move came at a time when, with a change from earlier opinion, it was thought fresh air offered a positive benefit to young babies.

A few perambulator companies, by this time, had already produced their first attempts at carriages for babies, but one of the first readily available options was based on the bassinet. These hooded wicker cradles, which were initially imported from France, were attached by a simple chassis to four wheels to create a flat-bed carriage. The introduction coincided with changes in the highway law that would now allow four-wheeled perambulators on public footpaths. This early version of a perambulator became known as a *bassinet*, and it soon evolved into a more sophisticated model fitted with a foot well to accommodate a sitting child.

A later, more sophisticated bassinet with a fitted foot well. The interior is lined with brown flannel and the handle is porcelain.

Even in the Victorian era major manufacturers found it worthwhile to produce a doll's version.

The popularity of carriages to carry babies encouraged manufacturers to produce a variety of new models. The bodies were still suspended on the same rigid chassis as the bassinet, but the use of shackles for attachment gave some limited flexing to improve the ride.

Many utilised the same basic tub shape as the bassinet but, being made of wood or papier mâché, they were more durable and weatherproof.

A simple box shape with foot well was, alternatively, used to create a variety of often ornate body profiles. Catalogues, in a clear link to horse-drawn carriages, sometimes referred to these prams as 'landaulettes'.

A recognisable feature on these early prams was the large oil box, with brass cap, on the wheels.

Wheel hub with oil box. The maker's name is clearly visible.

An elegant and very decorative pram made by Harrops of Stockport.

Right:
In deference to the widowed Queen Victoria, black was a popular colour choice but, as this small pram with its original paint shows, other colours were available.

 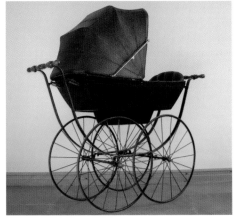

Above: The Simpson, Fawcett & Company single-sprung hammock pram was an important development. The body was suspended by leather straps from horizontal handles, which were, in their turn, attached to a single solid spring passing under the body.

Above: The progression from the single-sprung was the double-sprung hammock pram. The body was now suspended from two springs, giving more flexibility than the rather solid single spring.

The maker's name is cast into the axle in this view of the Simpson, Fawcett & Company single-sprung hammock pram

The perambulators shown so far had come a long way in providing a satisfactory carrier for babies that could also accommodate a growing toddler. The chassis, however, gave a far from smooth ride for the occupant and a better method of suspension was urgently needed. Simpson, Fawcett & Company, who made the prams illustrated on this page, and William Wilson, whose early pram appears later in the book, were among the pioneer spring smiths who developed and patented the first sprung chassis.

The final stage in the quest for an ideal method of suspension was the carriage hung by leather straps from two flexible 'cee' springs, but with the handle now attached directly to the body. This represented a major development, an innovation that would be used on nearly all carriage prams to the present day.

The concept and style of the Hitchings pram illustrated was so advanced that it would still be appropriate sixty years later. Hitchings, from whom the young Queen Victoria had bought her original three carriages, were considered to be the premier makers of quality prams at this time. A glance through their list of 'distinguished patrons' would reveal such entries as: 'Baby carriage for Baby Prince Edward of York', HRH the Duke of Edinburgh, HRH Princess Henry of Battenburg, and the royal families of Russia, Germany, Denmark, Portugal and Sweden.

Catalogues into the 1930s would still take a pride in the names of British and foreign royalty among their long list of patrons. The Empire and the spread of Queen Victoria's offspring throughout Europe were significant factors in the desire for British prams. More importantly, Britain had gained a reputation for expertise and quality in pram manufacture.

At home sales were booming but, interestingly, the owner of the little rustic cart shown in the first chapter remembered riding in it as a small child in the late Victorian period – a reminder that in rural communities, where family life was centred in the village and children played in the local fields, a perambulator may still have been regarded as an unaffordable and unnecessary luxury.

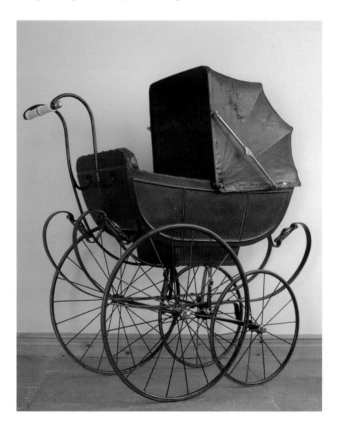

A perambulator made by Hitchings Ltd in the 1890s. It is a classic example of prams from that time.

By the early 1880s the parents and nannies of the Victorian era had been provided with a choice of three types of child's carriage; now a fourth also emerged.

The *mailcart*, as it was called, consisted of a usually decorative body supported by two large wheels and two stabilising wheels. It could, by adjusting the hinged foot well, be converted either to a flat bed or, alternatively, to seating for one or two toddlers. A major difference from the early three-wheeled carriage was that the occupant now faced the handles.

Below:
A painted wood mailcart configured as a flat

Above right:
A carved wood mailcart arranged to carry a sitting child.

Right:
A very different version of mailcart, known as the 'back to back', intended to carry two children.

An original Simpson, Fawcett & Company play cart.

Above:
The Royal Mail cart label.

Left :
An early mailcart that would carry a sitting child.

During the 1870s Simpson, Fawcett & Company had produced a two-wheeled cart 'to be used by boys and girls' to promote exercise, which they called 'The Royal Mailcart'. The cart obviously resembled the ones used for mail and was stamped 'Royal Mail' on the side rail. It was designed to be pulled along, with the side rails acting as shafts.

The cart had obvious potential for carrying younger children and similar carriages intended for that purpose soon followed. Unlike the original play carts, these mailcarts were pushed using curved shafts, and increasingly elaborate and creative variations on the style were made. The front stabilisers were now replaced by two small wheels, for safety reasons. They would evolve in a few years into the sophisticated carriages described on the previous page.

A variety of dolls' mailcarts was produced. They ranged from a simple cane seat set on a chassis to fine, detailed replicas of full-size convertible models. They were expensive and cherished possessions belonging to privileged children, who were expected to treat them with great care.

Mailcarts were made for only a short period (1880 to 1915) and for much of that time changed very little. Distinguishing between Victorian and Edwardian examples, particularly in dolls' models, can be difficult. Judged on style, the ones on this page should be Victorian.

A cane pram, c.1900, retailed by Hamley Bros Ltd.

Dolls' carriages had become, by the end of the era, an important part of the perambulator industry. Major manufacturers, including Harris and Leveson, produced doll's size versions with the same level of craftsmanship and attention to detail offered in their full-size models. Girls wanted a carriage that was just like the one their mother or nanny pushed, and pram companies were the obvious people to make them. The dolls' prams on this page and the next illustrate some of the styles and materials used at this time.

Below left:
A late Victorian carved and painted wood pram.

Below right:
A papier mâché double-sprung hammock pram.

The box shape much used in Victorian perambulators was particularly popular for dolls' carriages. The dolls' prams illustrate variations on this style that could, again, also be found in their full-size counterparts.

Picture postcards give a fascinating glimpse into the life of privileged Victorian girls with their prams. Postcards can be a useful aid in dating prams, especially when they carry a postmark.

A pram purchased from Hamleys, the famous London toy store.

A fine pram with an unusually ornate chassis.

The Jumeau doll is sitting in a pram made by W. J. Harris & Company.

A style of pram known as the 'rustic' or 'waggonette'.

The typically Victorian pram, with papier mâché body, is an exact replica of the one pictured on the postcard.

Small cane prams, like the one in the photograph above, were very popular toys. They often had a simple hood, as this typical example shows.

Beautiful pictures of Victorian families with their perambulators. The collection shows a mailcart, a double-sprung hammock pram and a doll's pram.

The Victorian era had brought rapid developments in baby-carriage design, from the production of the first three-wheeled victorias to bassinets, mailcarts and carriage perambulators. Pram manufacture in the Victorian era had become a major industry. Design was innovative and workmanship was of a high standard – each carriage was craftsman-built, with buttoned leather-cloth interior, brass fittings, coach-lined chassis and well-finished body.

Fortunes had been made and many famous names in manufacturing had emerged – Hitchings, Trotman, Dunkley, Leveson, Harris, and Simpson, Fawcett & Company, to name but a few. One curious success was George Hughes, who, having bought the patent for the Frampton metal wheel in 1880, had cornered the pram-wheel market and would continue to supply to most makers of prams for years to come.

Famous stores such as Harrods had commissioned and sold prams under their own name. Advertisements, along with manufacturers' and store catalogues, had given a further boost to an increasing trade.

Most significantly, the era had produced refined, practically designed carriages which future generations could modify and adapt to suit their needs and fashions.

The Victorian pram pictured is an appropriate model to represent the end of the era, having several features that would be seen as Edwardian fashion. The foot well, always visible below the body line in Victorian prams, was now less obvious. The pram, with its colour and ornate brasswork, symbolised a new sense of optimism at the turn of the century.

A decorative late Victorian pram with the interesting feature of a fold-down backrest.

EDWARDIAN STYLE

THE start of the Edwardian period, with an outward-going and more accessible monarch, brought a very different approach to living. It was to be an era of elegance and the pursuit of pleasure, and this was reflected in the style of perambulators that became popular.

The four types of carriage available at the end of the Victorian period would have different fortunes as fashions changed at the start of the twentieth century. The bassinet was already fast losing its appeal, whereas an ornate mailcart would, for a short period, be a particularly popular choice. The four-wheeled victoria would continue, but with styling appropriate to the new fashions.

The most noticeable change was in the style of the perambulator: the foot well was much less prominent and would soon be concealed by the sides of a canoe-shaped body. The overall appearance of the pram would present a pleasing picture of elegance. The period would come to be recognised by pram enthusiasts as one of the high points in pram design.

The appeal of Edwardian perambulators was often enhanced by brightly coloured paintwork, in direct contrast to the more sombre Victorian models. Vertical stripes in contrasting colours were a particular feature of the period and decorative cane work was popular for both prams and mailcarts.

The importance attached by an increasing number of families to owning a pram, and the best one affordable, is apparent in the many period photographs. A proud mother, or nanny, posing beside a beautifully dressed baby in the latest model of a carriage, complete with luxurious pram linen, was a popular subject for a picture.

Although the death of Edward VII in 1910 officially marked the end of the true Edwardian era, the influence of this period on baby-carriage design continued for some years longer. It would be the First World War that finally marked the point of radical change. Consequently this chapter is extended to cover the period from 1901 to 1918 and celebrates the abundance of beautiful perambulator models inspired by Edwardian style.

Opposite:
A studio photograph of a decorative Edwardian wicker and cane perambulator.

The four fine perambulators on this page and the next set the scene for this elegant era. The attractive style of Edwardian prams was complemented by the range of colours now considered desirable, but, as can be seen, many models were still made in sober colours. Nannies placed quality before flamboyance and since, by tradition, they were often allowed to choose the nursery pram, many dark colours were still sold. Nanny knew that, amongst her peers, she and the family would be judged by the quality of the pram when she went on her daily outings to the park.

Above: The symbol of a martlet on the side panels of this Edwardian carriage pram indicates that it belonged to the fourth son of an earl. The pram came from a terraced house in Bristol, perhaps the home of a proud nanny who had been presented with the pram when her duties were completed, as was often the custom.

Above: A post-Edwardian pram made by Marmet. The company was founded in 1912 and its prams are immediately recognisable by their method of suspension. The body is attached by coiled springs to a tubular chassis that wraps round it.

Below:
The calliper brake, just visible on the Marmet pram, first became available in the 1890s.

Above:
The martlet symbol on the side panel of the Edwardian carriage pram.

Left:
A classic post-Edwardian pram made by Sol. The dress guards, rarely seen in prams of its age, are celluloid and made by another well-known firm, Bluemels.

The prams illustrated are made by two of the leading companies of the day, although Hitchings were still considered to be the most prestigious of all. One significant development was that the porcelain handle, introduced in the late Victorian period, was in turn replaced. The handle now consisted of a simple wooden cylinder sheathed in either ebonite, a black vulcanised rubber coating, or Ivorine, a white celluloid-like material.

Below left:
A high-quality and popular pram by Hitchings. The white tyres were a feature of this model.

Below right:
The advertisement is taken from the 1909 Christmas issue of The Gentlewoman.

HITCHINGS' Ltd.
Under Royal Patronage.
Every Carriage built by HITCHINGS' Ltd. is a masterpiece in itself.
Please write for Illustrated Catalogue.
LONDON:
329, 331, OXFORD STREET, W.
(Corner of Bond Street).
45, KNIGHTSBRIDGE, S.W.
LIVERPOOL: 74, Bold Street.
MANCHESTER: 69, Deansgate.
GLASGOW: 1—174, Sauchiehall Street.

The convex side panels of this pram enhance the body shape and are a sign of quality.

A pram made by G. & J. Lines, with their thistle logo trademark. It was catalogued in 1909 as the 'Imperial' model.

The doll in this typically Edwardian pram is a Simon & Halbig 126.

The dolls' prams on this page, from the mid Edwardian period, reflect the changes seen in their full-size counterparts. The canoe-shaped body is much in evidence and the shadow stripes, often in shades of green, were popular at this time. Catalogues of dolls' prams did for a while, however, continue to offer, in addition, designs that seemed to belong to an earlier period.

A sweeping swan-neck style handle and the use of intricate cane and wicker work (see below) are typical of this period. The fashion for a decorative gallery around the body, along with cane scrolls and embellishments, is also well illustrated in these dolls' carriages. The larger wheels are 14 inches in diameter, as opposed to the 12 inches seen in most Victorian prams. Strangely, at a time when full-size models were using Ivorine or ebonite, dolls' prams often still had porcelain handles.

Below :
A particularly opulent pram with barley-twist fittings and burgundy leather cloth. The luxury of the pram is further enhanced by a clearly original buttoned plush interior of matching colour. The doll is a Kestner 211.

The umbrella holder is an interesting addition to this model made by Trotmans.

The Victorian design of the convertible mailcart had not changed, though, if anything, the Edwardian version had become even larger and more unwieldy. Nonetheless, with their ornate appearance, they seemed to match the spirit of the age and were very popular. The very decorative cane work and cornucopia are a sure sign that the mailcarts pictured on this page are Edwardian.

Above right:
A typical mailcart with all the features expected at this time.

Right:
A mailcart that could also be described as a perambulator – the tray slots in to make the conversion. It was one of a number of unusual designs in vogue in the late Edwardian period. The crossbar that joins the shafts was introduced to improve safety and is fitted on later mailcarts.

A detailed doll's replica of a post-Edwardian mailcart.

Mailcarts, which had been so popular at the beginning of the new century, were, in the post-Edwardian period, already losing their appeal. The ornate wicker models were replaced by a more functional, pram-like design with wooden bodies.

The accurately modelled doll's version illustrates the change. It can still be converted, using a hinged tray, from a flat bed to a sitting mode and the occupant still faces the handle, justifying its definition as a mailcart. However, it bears little resemblance to its former counterpart and, even with such a radical redesign, virtually none would be made after 1918.

A doll's convertible model, retailed by Gamages, similar to the full-size one shown on the previous page. It is also shown with the tray removed to create a sitting pram.

Victorias had seen some limited modifications in styling to suit current fashions but the basic concept was unchanged from that seen at the end of the Victorian period. They looked as though they provided a cosy and comfortable ride for the young occupants and they continued to find customers.

A top-quality model, as would be expected, from Fred McKenzie, International Baby Carriage Company, one of the leading manufacturers of the period.

Right:
The rather less expensive victoria offers plenty of room to accommodate a growing child. It would have comfortably carried a five-year-old.

Far right:
A simple doll's version available at this time.

A doll's version. Without the occupant, it could well be taken as a child's size model.

Small cane 'carriages', as shown by period postcards, became popular during the Edwardian period. They would have been described as victorias but can also be seen as early forerunners of the pushchair. They were attractive, compact, and very practical for carrying toddlers, and this must have contributed to the eventual loss in popularity of the much larger mailcart.

Period postcards showing fashion in perambulators and dress, and giving a nostalgic snapshot of Edwardian society.

The years between the end of Edward VII's reign and the First World War had seen a move away from the attractive, colourful prams so popular in the early years of the twentieth century. The drab appearance of the pram illustrated and the slight change in profile are the first indicators of greater changes to come. This model would still have been available in 1918, until new post-war models could be introduced.

The era had seen the first use of tangent-spoke ball-bearing wheels and, in the last years, bodies built of three-ply timber. Also during the period leading up to the war, with increasing use of mass-production methods, prams became ever more affordable for a wider section of the community.

The Edwardian period would be remembered as a time of elegant canoe-shaped prams and

A solidly made but basic pre-war child's pram.

ornate mailcarts. The war, however, put an end to this memorable period in perambulator production. The mailcart would not be seen again, ousted by more functional alternatives, and it would be another fifty years before prams once again enjoyed the same reputation for elegance.

A post-Edwardian doll's perambulator.

35

BETWEEN THE WARS

A LARGE deep-bodied pram is an immediately recognisable image of the 1920s and 1930s. The shape of prams in this era could not have been in greater contrast to the high canoe-shaped designs of the Edwardian era. Small wheels and low-slung square bodies were the new fashion. The style, which began to appear after the First World War, reached its extreme by the end of the 1920s, before a return to more conventional models in the mid 1930s.

There were good logical reasons for this new style, particularly the need for a stable and secure pram to protect a precious post-war generation. It was also the case that current medical opinion recommended the need for children to have regular daytime periods of rest in the fresh air, and where better to achieve these aims than a roomy and cosy pram in the garden?

The era would, along with changes in body style, bring significant developments in suspension and wheel technology. Folding pushchairs and prams would become popular as the needs of a new generation were met. Most families would expect to own a perambulator, so the market would need to adapt to offer prams that were both less expensive and suited to more modest accommodation.

Opposite:
An early 1920s Marmet doll's pram with an Armand Marseille 'My Dream Baby' doll.

Right:
The mid-era photograph of a well-dressed family shows that deep-bodied prams could look attractive and in harmony with the fashions of their day.

In the years immediately following the First World War prams were in a transitional stage between the new 1920s style and the old Edwardian one. The body had become deeper and was no longer canoe-shaped but, with relatively large wheels, the pram still managed to give the appearance of a high coach-built carriage. Nonetheless, with bodies now made from plywood and nickel-plated fittings, these early post-war models already carried some of the features to be incorporated in the new era of pram production.

Left: The full-size pram is made by Stone & Sons of Stoke Newington. The wheels are 20 inches and 14 inches in diameter. The black pram is lined with brown leather cloth. The new practice of lining the hood with matching leather cloth is evident.

Above: The good-quality doll's pram from the same period reflects changes happening in full-size models. At some point in its history it has lost its hood. The doll is a Heubach Koppelsdorf 302.

Perambulators in the early 1920s continued to be a hybrid of the old and the new designs. The body had already taken on the new deep square shape, characteristic of prams of this era. However, the method of suspension was as yet unchanged, with the cee springs still being attached to supports under the ends of the body. The wheel size had been reduced to manage the increased depth of the body.

Treasure Cot C⁰ Lᵗᵈ

SPRING EXHIBITION

in our New Showrooms
of the leading makes of

BABY CARRIAGES

from £6 10 0 to £31 10 0

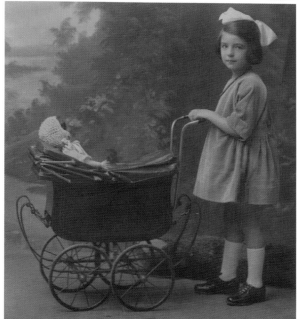

Above left:
The Dunkley pram is huge, having a body length of 42 inches and depth of 22 inches. The depth of the inside bed is 13 inches, making the pram both safe and secure for the occupant.

Above right:
A Treasure Cot advertisement from 1922, showing a very similar pram.

Left:
A contemporary picture of a girl proud of her doll's pram and doll.

The prams illustrated here are very similar to those shown on the previous page but differ in one significant feature. The introduction of 'cranked', or offset, cee springs allowed the carriage to be supported by rods that now passed through the body. The advantage of this innovation was that the body could be lowered without increasing the width of the wheelbase. The step was important in providing a more stable and safer pram.

Left: This pram, made by Fred McKenzie, International Baby Carriage Company, gives a good illustration of the first cranked cee springs. The carriage is fitted with a drop-down foot extension, giving an increase in the overall bed length when required.

Above:
This doll's pram with similar springs is made by Sillers of Leeds. It differs from the McKenzie pram in having improved, tangent-spoke wheels with broad Sorbo tyres.

Right:
This Treasure Cot advertisement from a 1924 magazine confirms that cranked cee springs were being used on prams at this time. Comparison with the same firm's advertisement on the previous page shows how much had changed in two years.

The
Treasure Carriage

The Treasure Carriage

Call and Inspect

or write for Catalogue.

There is no other like it. It is strong, safe and roomy, delightful in appearance, light, and very easy running. Can be supplied in any colour desired.

PRICES :—

Grade A.	Grade B.	Grade C.
£10:5:0	£13:13:0	£18:10:0

Perambulators had, by the mid 1920s, incorporated most of the new approaches to pram design. Bodies were generally deep and square, though the extremes to which this style was taken varied. The cee springs were neatly cranked, by shaping the metal, and attached by straps to rods passing through the body. The wheels were small, compared to previous fashion, and fitted with tangential spokes to increase strength. The rims were now broad to accommodate the thick Sorbo rubber tyres, producing a softer ride. The combined effect of wheel and cee-spring changes was, even with the deep body, to lower the height of a pram. The reduced height was designed not only to make for easier access but also, in lowering the centre of gravity, to create a more stable pram, one almost impossible to topple by even the most boisterous four-year-old. The other obvious change was that, after a short period of nickel plating, all metal fittings were now chromium-plated.

A fine pram from the mid 1920s. It was made by Leveson and has all the hallmarks of quality. The body is deep, as expected in this era, but, in keeping with the work of many top manufacturers, is not too exaggerated, managing to maintain a pleasing style. It has a drop-down foot extension to increase further the size of an already large pram, creating a bed length of 4 feet. A foot extension was often included as an optional extra on quality prams of this type. The reversible hood has a silk lining and frilling lace to back and front, with a black rubber-duck covering. Chrome is used on all fittings, including the decorative acorn-shaped finials and Leveson-style handle arms.

A doll's version of the 'Glyda'. It is an exact replica of the full-size model.

THE **GLYDA**
Pat. Nos. 22368/241609/245180
MARMET Ltd., LETCHWORTH.
ENGLAND.

The Marmet trade mark label on the Glyda pram.

Above left:
Detail of the 'Glyda' patent sponge-rubber suspension.

The Marmet Company, set up by E. T. Morris only a few years earlier, in 1912, was to become one of the major producers of popular prams in this era. Its familiar wrap-round, or Morris, chassis could be configured to suit most body shapes and Marmet produced a wide range of differing models and styles, both in full and doll's size carriages.

The 'Glyda' model, introduced in the mid 1920s, was, however, a notable exception. It was described and patented as the first 'chassisless' pram. The springing was provided by sponge-rubber shock absorbers surrounding the axle where it passed through the body. The effect of the system was to lower the height of the pram and, with no metal chassis, to reduce the weight. The name 'Glyda' could be justified by the description 'It glides along at the slightest touch'. The new method of suspension was also claimed to make the 'Glyda' the easiest of all to push and guide.

Sol were meanwhile producing their own answer to the low, well-sprung chassis. The patent 'Sol-no-jar' pram chassis cleverly provided a way of attaching the axles using a second layer of springs.

The page from a 1928 catalogue showing the 'Dainty' states that the pram, costing £12 18s 0d, offered such features as a body of best birch three-ply, a hood with corner shields and broad frilling hood lace, and wheels of 12 inches with tangent spokes on white rubber Sol tyres. The safety belt, 'affording a maximum of liberty of movement with absolute security', cost an extra 2 shillings.

The Sol 'Dainty' is a good example of an attractive deep-bodied pram. The claret colour was available at an additional cost of 4 shillings, the fine lines in gold for 2s 8d, and an extra coat of fine varnish cost 7 shillings.

The "Sol" Safety-bend hood-joints prevent torn dresses and hurt hands. Registered and Patent Application accepted.

THE "DAINTY."
(Patent Nos. 139433 and 224390.
Registration No. 706142.)

BODY of best birch three-ply, 36 inches long, three detachable cushions. Tubular levers and patent "Sol-no-jar" springs stove-enamelled. Handle celluloid. Hood with corner-shields originally registered, and broad frilling lace. Water proof apron with "Sol" storm - screen. Upholstery piped. Wheels 12 inch with tangent spokes and ⅞-inch white rubber "Sol" tyres,

£11 9 0.

The "DAINTY" for twins,
£12 18 0.

Larger twin carriages are listed on page 23.
Ball-bearing wheels **13/4** extra.
Every Carriage Guaranteed Perfect, Artistic, Durable and Cheap.

43

Top left:
A high-quality
Leeway pram with
Art Deco
moulding.

Top right:
A large and
attractive pram
showing a
variation on the
deep-bodied style.
Similar full-size
models were made.

Dolls' prams reflected the styles and features also seen in full-size models in the late 1920s. The wheels were small and usually had dress guards, while the standard deep body style appeared in a variety of shapes. The hood levers, for a short period, had a ribbed rubber coating. Tri-ang, which commanded a major share of the market, became, in 1929, the first company to use metal for pram bodies. All their models from this time on would be made from metal, using a production-line process that allowed the company to market prams at increasingly affordable prices.

An example of the
new metal-bodied
range of Tri-ang
prams. Notice the
space-saving fold-
down handle.

Folding wooden pushchairs were first made in the late Edwardian period and continued, little changed, into the 1920s. They were often available for hire at seaside railway stations for use by the visiting holidaymakers. Folding metal and canvas pushchairs were a later development and produced by several companies to varying levels of sophistication. Some were very basic, but practical and inexpensive.

Right:
This pushchair was used for hire in Victoria Park, Bath.

Below:
This studio photograph is a charming record of an early 1920s folding pushchair.

Below right:
A Tri-ang folding metal and canvas pushchair with a Heubach Koppelsdorf 300 doll.

The following two pages illustrate fine carriage prams made by some of the leading manufacturers of this period. These quality models were often passed from one generation to the next. Millsons' brochure, like many others at the time, stated: 'Repairs and renovations of any description to customer's specification undertaken, and carriages are loaned free of charge while repairs, etc., are being effected.' The quality and make of the family baby carriage was so important that job advertisements for nannies would often quote the make of the pram.

Top left:
A Millsons 'Featherweight' pram of the mid 1920s with a birch-wood body, sheathed in aluminium. The carriage is still suspended from under-body supports. Millsons' catalogue at this time showed both systems of body suspension in use.

Top right:
The Oxford Street address confirms that this model was made before Millsons' move to Wigmore Street in the 1930s.

A Pedigree pram appropriately named the 'Luxury'. Pedigree was part of the Tri-ang group of companies, so this would be one of their last models to be made with the traditional wooden body.

Above left:
A relatively compact model made by Sol, with a foot extension. It is a good example of the changing style of prams.

Above right:
This mid-1930s pram made by Hitchings was used continuously by the same family for more than thirty years. A balancing axle can be seen on the pram.

Left:
A Marmet pram from the late 1930s – the model was still being advertised in the immediate post-war period.

In the early 1930s prams returned to a more traditional style, set higher and with less deep bodies. Again, medical opinion played a part in this move by advising that very deep prams did not allow sufficient circulation of air.

A major safety innovation at this time was the introduction on all prams of a brake, operated by a foot lever. Larger prams were often also fitted with a balancing axle to adjust the length of the wheelbase when a second child was carried at the handle end.

Right:
A 1930s victoria
made by Sol. A
similar model was
still available for
purchase in the
1950s.

Far right:
An earlier version
of the Sol,
complete with
original leather-
cloth storm apron.

Victorias remained popular during this period and were listed in the catalogues of all the top manufacturers, where they were described as 'A roomy sitting up car suitable for a child up to five years of age'.

Many offered the alternatives of a handle-facing model or, in true victoria style, the handle-at-back type.

Victorias were particularly popular with families able to afford a nanny. Among the general public, however, they were already in competition with the very practical and less expensive pushchair.

The victoria
illustrated in
Millsons' 1930
catalogue.

A full-size pram retailed by the Treasure Cot Company. The company employed many of the top manufacturers to produce prams under its name. The style of this one suggests it was made by the Marmet company. The pram has a mohair hood and apron, this fabric then being offered by Treasure Cot as an alternative to rubber duck or leather cloth.

The shapely carriage pram illustrated is from the late 1930s and shows the continuing trend towards the return of the large canoe-style body. The pre-eminence of such prams was, however, being challenged by some practical alternatives. The soft-bodied folding pram had been available since the 1920s and a small drop-toe pramette, with folding handle, was already being advertised in manufacturers' 1939 catalogues. Both would be available after the Second World War, with the pramette becoming particularly popular in the 1950s.

The start of war meant that this would be, for most companies, the last opportunity to showcase their new models for some years.

Pram companies would be taken over to support the war effort and this, combined with a shortage of raw materials, would mean that the supply of new prams would be very limited. Many prams from the 1930s would still be in use beyond the end of the war, having been passed to family or friends, or bought second-hand.

The expectation of pram ownership had, in the last twenty years, extended to all families. While the war would bring a temporary pause to the industry, the benefits of newly acquired technology and skills offered a promising future for pram production in the 1950s.

Silver Cross

The world's most exclusive

BABY COACH

A POST-WAR REVIVAL

THE end of the Second World War was a difficult and challenging time for industry, with its main focus for the last six years suddenly removed. Pram manufacturers had been among the companies co-opted to support the war effort and this proved for some to be a valuable experience. They now found themselves with newly learned techniques and production methods that could equally be applied to pram manufacture. The potential existed for well-made, mass-produced prams at a reasonable price, but materials were in short supply and it would take time to create designs that would capitalise on these new procedures. Silver Cross, in particular, having been employed by the Air Ministry during the war, would convert to pressed metal for all their future pram bodies. Such was the quality and popularity of their products and designs that Silver Cross continues to be the name most associated with fine prams to the present day. Marmet, the other major name of the era, were less influenced by the new technology but, with a succession of attractive models, would still find wide appeal. Many of the pre-war traditional pram companies continued to produce quality coach-built prams for wealthier customers.

Production was slow to resume after the war, with very few new models introduced, but rapidly recovered in the early 1950s. Led by a resurgent Silver Cross, manufacturers vied to produce catalogues showing new attractive models. The Coronation of Queen Elizabeth II in 1953 proved to be a watershed for a country celebrating an end to years of austerity and was an incentive for pram companies to advertise new models. The advertisements were keen to link the pram with this great royal occasion. High carriage prams were back in fashion, starting a trend that would peak in the 1960s.

Opposite:
The 1955 Silver Cross advertisement from *Country Life* magazine was one of a series produced in the 1950s featuring Rolls Royces in the background.

Below:
A Coronation year advertisement by Osnath.

"THE LONDON"

Osnath

The Baby Carriage for
A GREAT OCCASION

Every feature, from its restrained and dignified design to its balanced springing and ease of propulsion, bespeaks a standard of excellence which has become an Osnath tradition.

Osnath
Easily the best since the days of Victoria

Write for Catalogue in Full Colour
ASHTON BROS. & PHILLIPS LTD., WARRINGTON, LANCS.

A Tri-ang doll's
pram with leather
cloth upholstery.

The style of prams immediately after the war showed little change from 1939, with many companies still selling their pre-war models. A lack of raw materials, such as plywood and steel, meant that not enough new prams could be made to meet demand. The models that manufacturers were able to produce were often, of necessity, lacking in luxury and were known as utility prams. Nonetheless, the news that a local retailer had 'managed to find' a few prams would quickly spread and there would be a rush of eager customers.

The prams illustrated are from the immediate post-war period and clearly reflect the designs of the late 1930s. A telling feature was the continued use of leather cloth for upholstery, but, affected by wartime shortages, it was often of inferior quality, being sticky to the touch. Plastic material replaced leather cloth in the early 1950s.

A pair of pre-
1950s metal
Leeway prams.

The *pramette* and the *folder*, two similar styles of adaptable pram, found favour in the post-war period. Both offered an easy conversion from a standard flat bed for babies to a sitting position for toddlers, with extra leg room.

The pramette had a hard body and, though first advertised in the late 1930s, was at its most popular in the 1950s, with many companies producing their own version of the system. These prams were generally compact, with a foldaway handle, and in some models the body could be detached from the low chassis.

The cloth-bodied folder was made from the late 1920s to the early 1970s and remained popular throughout that period. The body could be folded for ease of transport. These prams, also, often had a lift-off body and were variously described as 'pram cots' or 'bed cars', reflecting their dual-purpose advantages.

Far left:
A pramette, with wooden body made by Swan.

Left:
This Marmet folder was purchased new in 1972. The company had first catalogued a folding pram in 1928.

An early leather-cloth folding doll's pram, from the 1930s.

Silver Cross had been much influenced by their wartime experience and set about applying their acquired knowledge of pressed-metal technology to a new generation of prams. They produced a succession of attractive designs in full and doll's size models.

Silver Cross doll's prams from the 1950s with a variety of attractive mouldings. The lower two are examples of a model called 'Jean'.

The 1950s range of dolls' prams was a good example of their work at this time and justified their description as 'the world's most exclusive dolls' carriages'. They were a detailed three-quarters scale version of the company's early 1950s full-size models and were produced in two qualities, Standard and Super. Each of the different designs was given a girl's name. Prices ranged from £10 to £15.

The 'Versailles' model, first produced by Wilson Silver Cross in the late 1950s, is one of the best-remembered post-war perambulators. It was in the traditional carriage style with distinctive body shape and attractive moulding. The larger wheels varied in size from 20 inches to 24 inches in diameter.

Detail of the rose plaque decoration on the full and doll's size prams.

The advertisement shows the Silver Cross 'Versailles' model, which was decorated with a hand-painted swag of flowers. Other models using the same body shape included the 'Monaco' with ceramic rose plaque (shown above), the 'Antibes', which had a similar plaque depicting a bird of paradise, a model with a Wedgwood plaque depicting a mother and child, and the 'Pastorale', which was painted with an overall pattern of small sprigs of flowers.

A typical LBC
pram with a foot
extension.

The London Baby
Coach Company
had a relatively
short history. It
was founded in the
1920s and taken
over by Marmet in
the 1960s.

The demand for traditional coach-built prams in the 1950s could still support a small group of companies specialising in this market. The London Baby Coach Company (LBC) produced a limited range of high-quality models to attract discerning customers. Other firms specialising in this field were Osnath, Millsons and Davies. The term 'coach-built' was used to define prams made of wood as opposed to the general term 'carriage', which could be applied to all prams of this style, whether of metal or of wood.

The LBC carriage illustrated has many of the features expected in 1950s prams. The larger wheels are 22 inches in diameter, compared to the 24 inch wheels favoured in the 1960s. The body is canoe-shaped and, like many of these prams, has a foot extension – growing children still enjoyed a rest period in the garden.

The LBC Company, like the other renowned manufacturers mentioned, did not survive beyond the 1960s, either being taken over or simply closing down.

The 1960s was the last decade in which the family pram was seen as a major outlay and source of pride. High on the wish list of many mothers was the Marmet 'Queen'. The pram was an expensive luxury but, with a contribution from fond grandparents, it could be just affordable. It is still regarded by many as one of the most beautiful prams ever made and, to this day, commands a high price when resold. The elegantly shaped body, set high on 24 inch and 20 inch wheels, marked a complete return to a style first seen in the Edwardian period.

The 'Queen' signalled an end to the use of the wrap-round chassis that had, for so long, been a unique characteristic of Marmet prams. The company logo on the pram proudly states 'Marmet coach built'.

The quality of finish, the profile and style of this model combined to produce one of the iconic prams of the era. It was in production from the late 1950s to the early 1970s.

The 'Queen of baby carriages', as it was described in Marmet's catalogue, was a pram of luxury and refinement. The specifications included an interior zip-fastener pocket in the side panel and the option of a pocket-end foot extension. The body was mounted on roller bearings and there was a specially designed Marmet hand brake de luxe. The original owner of the carriage saved sixpences all through her pregnancy to afford her dream pram.

The 'London'
model with
'Osnath silk' hood
and apron. The
perambulator cost
34 guineas (£35
14s) in 1963.

The Osnath pram company, which had been in business since the Victorian era, produced a very fine range of high coach-built prams in the 1950s and early 1960s. The company was renowned for the quality and finish of the paintwork on the wooden bodies. Its catalogue stated: 'In their production there is more than labour, more than craftsmanship – there is that indefinable something that makes them different from, and better than, any other Baby Coaches you can buy.' They were further described as 'the Rolls-Royce of the pavement'.

The graceful
Osnath 'Duchess'
with swan-neck
handles. It is an
earlier model with
22 inch and 18
inch wheels.

A model by Millsons called the 'Prince', with its 22 inch and 24 inch wheels. The 'Prince' had the unusual feature of a small storage compartment set below the foot extension.

Millsons, in an era of change, managed always to retain their reputation for producing 'the most exclusive prams'. They had inherited the mantle from Hitchings in the 1920s and, like that company, could claim many famous and royal customers. Distinguished patrons had ranged from the 150 titled ladies listed in their 1930 brochure to, more recently, Queen Elizabeth II.

The prams were always expensive but this was matched by the high quality of workmanship and, of course, the distinction of owning a Millsons pram. Their catalogue significantly promised: 'Every Millsons Carriage has the name on the handle bar and our name plate on the back panel.'

The company produced in the 1950s and 1960s large, impressive prams in the traditional style.

A twin version of the famous 'Cavendish' model.

The Pedigree pram illustrated in this 1953 advertisement had a system whereby two stabilisers were lowered when the brake was applied.

This is luxury

—comfort, style and safety that delights the most exacting taste
The Clarence by Pedigree.

Pedigree
REGD. TRADE MARK

Royale were among the leading pram manufacturers of this era, claiming the title 'the world's most beautiful baby coach'.

Both full and doll's size models now had metal bodies. The prams had their own distinctive style, the most recognisable feature being the use of coiled springs to connect the body to the chassis.

Pedigree had been using metal for pram bodies since the late 1920s and continued to make attractive, competitively priced prams until the late 1960s.

Right:
A typical 1960s Royale full-size pram.

Far right:
A Royale doll's pram. The matching bag was a popular accessory at the time.

Far left:
A Marmet pram
with lift-off body.
The corduroy
fabric and rounded
hood were a
popular choice.

Left:
An attractive Silver
Cross model with
metal lift-off body.

This Silver Cross
doll's pram, called
the 'Gaye', was a
copy of the full-
size 'Parkward'.

Silver Cross had, in the late 1960s, introduced their new range of carriage prams, including the 'Silver Shadow', 'Mulliner' and 'Parkward', all names associated with Rolls-Royce. The body had become shallower and the suspension changed slightly in that the rods now passed under the body, rather than through it. The body appeared to sit very high and, with 24 inch and 18 inch wheels, the pram had a style of its own. Marmet were, at this time, producing a similar pram.

In the 1970s Silver Cross and Marmet also introduced a new range of prams with lift-off bodies. They were more easily accommodated in a motor vehicle and reflected the fact that most families now owned a car. They offered a modern version of the carriage pram but with the convenience of a folding chassis for easy stowage. There was a choice of either steel or fabric bodies. New modern fabrics were available: nylon corduroy was a popular choice for soft-bodied prams at this time.

One of the models in the 2008 Silver Cross Lifestyle Solutions range, the 'Sleepover Deluxe Classic'.

The Maclaren buggy, with its lightweight tubular aluminium collapsible chassis and small swivel wheels arranged in four pairs, marked a radical rethink in pram design. First produced in the late 1970s, it was the forerunner of the modern cloth-bodied multi-use systems that have dominated the pram market since the late 1980s.

The very latest 'package with one click' models can variously provide an overnight carry-cot, a protective pram, a reversible pushchair or a car seat. The whole is designed to meet the needs of modern living.

Imported models take a significant share of this market but, in keeping with the rest of this book, the ones shown on this page are British, having been produced by Silver Cross.

A 1998 Silver Cross Toy 'Ultima' 2 in 1 combination, with sun canopy.

The 1997 doll's version of the 'Wayfarer Combo' in pushchair mode, with a PVC rain-hood.

THE WAY FORWARD

BABY carriages have, for more than 150 years, continuously evolved to suit the changing lifestyles and fashions of the era in which they were made. A thriving post-war industry has, however, gradually declined, with many manufacturers unable to adapt to change. Once-famous names in pram production have disappeared as their coach-built prams, so favoured in the 1960s, were no longer suited to modern needs.

Silver Cross is the one name to survive from the post-war generation of pram manufacturers and provides a fitting end to this book. The company, set up by William Wilson in 1877, has been the one constant through the four eras of pram production. William Wilson was, in his time at the factory, responsible for thirty design patents, the first being the double-sprung hammock system. It has been that spirit of innovation and adaptability that has allowed the company to survive to this day.

A major part of the Silver Cross business now lies with the modern pram systems, but they continue to find a ready market for their traditional carriage prams, which are still made in Yorkshire and British.

Far left:
The William Wilson double-sprung hammock pram made in 1878.

Left:
A 2007 model in the Silver Cross Heritage range, called the 'Balmoral'.

INDEX

Armand Marseille doll 3, 36
ambrotype 10
'Antibes' (Silver Cross) 55

back to back (mailcart) 16
back rest 23
'Balmoral' (Silver Cross) 63
bassinet 4, 12, 23, 25
Bath chair 7, 9
Bluemels 27

calliper brake 26
cane 19, 21, 25, 29, 30, 33
cart 7
'Cavendish' (Millsons) 59
'cee' springs 15, 39, 40, 41
chromium plate 41
cornucopia, cane 30
cranked springs 40

'Dainty' (Sol) 43
Davies 56
dress guards 27, 44
'Duchess' (Osnath) 58
Dunkley 23, 39

ebonite 27, 29

folder (pram) 53
Fred McKensie 32, 40
Frampton 11, 23
foot lever brake 47
foot extension 40, 41, 56

Gamages 31
'Glyda' (Marmet) 42

Hamleys 20
Hamley Bros Ltd 19
hammock pram 14, 19, 22
Hampshire, Jack 4
Harris, W. J. 19, 20, 23
Harrods 4, 23
Harrops 13
Heubach Kopplesdorf doll 38, 45
Hitchings Ltd 15, 23, 27, 47, 59
hood lace 41, 43
Hughes, George 23

International Baby Carriage Company 32, 40
Ivorine 27, 29

Kestner doll 29

leather cloth 10, 23, 38, 49, 52, 53
Leeway 44, 52
Lines, G. & J. 28
London Baby Coach 56
'London' (Osnath) 58

Maclaren buggy 62
mailcart, doll's 3, 5, 18, 31
mailcart, full size 8, 16, 17, 22, 25, 30, 33, 35
Marmet 4, 26, 36, 42, 47, 49, 51, 53, 56, 57, 61
Martlet 26
Millsons 46, 48, 56, 59
mohair fabric 49
'Monaco' (Silver Cross) 55

Morris, E.T. 42
'Mulliner' (Silver Cross) 61

nickel plating 38, 41

oil box 13
Osnath 51, 56, 58

papier mache 13, 19, 21
park carriage 6
'Parkward' (Silver Cross) 61
'Pastorale' (Silver Cross) 55
Pedigree 46, 60
plywood 35, 38, 42
porcelain handle 12, 27, 29
pramette 49, 53
'Prince' (Millsons) 59
pushchair 33, 37, 45

'Queen' (Marmet) 57

Royale 60
Royal Mail Cart 17
rubber duck 41, 49
'Rustic' pram 20

safety straps 10, 43
Scowens 10
shackle 13
shadow stripes 28
Silver Cross 50, 51, 54, 55, 61, 62, 63
'Silver Shadow' (Silver Cross) 61
Simon and Halbig doll 28
Simpson, Fawcett & Co. 14, 17, 23
'Sleepover' (Silver Cross) 62

Sol 27, 43, 47, 48
Sorbo rubber tyre 40, 41
Stone and Sons 38
sun canopy 10
swan pram 53

tangent spoke wheel 35, 40, 41
Treasure Cot 39, 40, 49
Tri-ang 44, 45, 46, 52
Trotmans 10, 23, 30

'Ultima' (Silver Cross) 62
umbrella holder 30

'Versailles' (Silver Cross) 55
victoria carriage 11, 25, 32, 33, 48

waggonette 20
'Wayfarer' (Silver Cross) 62
Wedgwood plaque 55
wicker 12, 25, 29, 31
Wilson Silver Cross 55
Wilson, William 14, 63